# SIMPLE PRAYERS FOR HURTING PEOPLE

*Conversing with God in the Midst of Pain*

By Terence B. Lester

SIMPLE PRAYERS FOR HURTING PEOPLE
© 2013 by Terence B. Lester
Printed by U-Turn Books, LLC.

All rights reserved. No part of this book may be reproduced, stored in a retrieval system, or transmitted in any form or by any means—electronic, mechanical, photocopy, recording or otherwise—without the written permission of the publisher, except for brief quotations in printed reviews.

Scripture taken from the Holy Bible, New International Version®. Copyright © 1973, 1978, 1984 International Bible Society. Used by permission of Zondervan. All rights reserved.

Scripture quotations marked "ESV" are from the ESV Bible® (The Holy Bible, English Standard Version®), copyright © 2001 by Crossway Bibles, a publishing ministry of Good News Publishers. Used by permission. All rights reserved.

Scripture quotations marked "NRSV" are taken from the New Revised Standard Version Bible, copyright 1989, Division of Christian Education of the National Council of the Churches of Christ in the United States of America. Used by permission. All rights reserved.

Scripture quotations marked NKJV™ are taken from the New King James Version®. Copyright © 1982 by Thomas Nelson, Inc. Used by permission. All rights reserved.

ISBN: 978-0615837130

Printed in the United States of America

# Table of Contents

Dedication ..................................................................... v

Preface ........................................................................ vii

1. Prayer about Uncertainty ........................................ 1
2. Prayer about Worry ................................................. 3
3. Prayer about Doubt ................................................. 5
4. Prayer for Strength ................................................. 7
5. Prayer about Second-Guessing ............................... 9
6. Prayer for Provision .............................................. 11
7. Prayer for a Miracle .............................................. 13
8. Prayer about Anxiety ............................................ 17
9. Prayer for Direction .............................................. 19
10. Prayer about Rejection .......................................... 23
11. Prayer about Disappointment ................................ 25
12. Prayer about Sensitivity and Emotions ................. 27
13. Prayer about Over-Thinking ................................. 29
14. Prayer about Quitting ........................................... 31
15. Prayer about Being Misunderstood ....................... 35
16. Prayer about Isolation .......................................... 37
17. Prayer about Betrayal ........................................... 39
18. Prayer for Relationships ....................................... 43

19. Prayer about Sorrow ................................................45

20. Prayer about Emptiness............................................47

21. Prayer for Forgiveness .............................................49

22. Prayer about Acceptance..........................................51

23. Prayer for Rest and Peace ........................................53

24. Prayer about People Pleasing ...................................55

25. Prayer about Busyness .............................................59

26. Prayer about Blaming ...............................................63

27. Prayer about Envy and Comparison .........................65

28. Prayer to Find My Way Home..................................67

29. Prayer about Depression ..........................................69

30. Prayer for Counsel ...................................................71

31. Prayer for Wisdom...................................................73

32. Prayer for Family ....................................................75

33. Prayer for Hope.......................................................77

34. Prayer for Healing ...................................................79

35. Prayer to Let Go......................................................81

36. Prayer of Confession................................................83

37. Prayer about Conflict ...............................................85

38. Prayer about Grief...................................................87

39. Prayer for Endurance ...............................................89

40. Prayer about Process ...............................................91

41. Prayer for Personal Growth .....................................93

Walking With God through Christ................................95

*I dedicate this book to all of the people who have not known how to communicate with God in the midst of their suffering. May God hear you and answer your deepest prayers and concerns!*

# *Preface*

Have you ever been too hurt to pray? Have you ever known your true feelings but were ashamed to share them with God? Or have you every started out really great in your relationship with God, but something bad happened along the way to keep you from getting closer to God? Maybe life knocked you down, maybe you hit a pothole of failure, maybe you experienced a wound in church, or maybe God did not answer a prayer you desperately needed God to answer—and because of these things, you became upset or mad with God to the point you never wanted to speak with God again!

If this is you, I can relate to that experience! In fact, life has knocked me down time and again. Life has hit me so hard that I never thought I would speak to God again through prayer! "Pray to God for what," I thought. "He doesn't answer anyway!" I followed with my other smart remark: "So what if God knows my thoughts afar off!"

I wasn't going to open my heart again in prayer! Why? Because of the pain and hurt! I was too hurt to pray! And guess what? When you are too hurt to pray, prayer can sometimes be the last thing on your mind. However, being in this place is really hard because, not only do you close yourself off to God, but you close yourself off to people, the world, and yourself. Not a good place, huh? However, after being in this place for a year, I became really desperate and in need of a release.

I needed to speak to someone—anyone—because I was not opening up to anyone (not even my closest friends)! If you have ever felt silenced to the point that it is not healthy, then you understand what I am talking about. My misunderstanding caused me to blame God for where I was and accuse him of not being where I wanted to be. Is this you? Can you relate? I literally tried to push myself away from God by remaining silent, and now I needed to talk to God to restore me. Funny, huh? Isn't it amazing that, when we try to cut ourselves off from the very one who supplies life, we quickly see how we cannot go on without life? This caused me to see that there is no life apart from God.

The silence contributed to my distance from God in prayer, and I was tired of the distance.

When I got tired of that distance, something happened. Something inside me longed to connect with God again through prayer—the main source of life! It was one verse in the book of Isaiah that pushed me over the edge and caused me to begin praying again: *"He gives power to the weak and to those who have no might he increases strength"* (Isaiah 40:29).

I quickly realized that, if I were to gain strength from the blows I received in life, I would have to reconnect with God through prayer. I was broken and in desperate need of the power, strength, and life God gives to weak people.

There are many books out there on prayer in the Christian tradition. They will teach you steps to praying, why praying is important, how you can pray prayers to get God to answer you, and a number of other different topics. This is not that type of book! Let me caution you! This book is comprised of several different journal prayers that helped me to start back talking to God through prayer. In it, you will find prayers for when I'm excited and prayers for when I'm in doubt. You'll find prayers for when I seem desperate and prayers for when I need God to build me up.

If you are broken, you will relate. I decided to turn my journal into a book because I realized that I am not the only one who has struggled with trying to connect with God or find the right words to say when I was hurting after life had knocked me down. I am not promising you that this book will help God answer your prayers! I'm simply sharing my prayers in hopes that they help you start back on a path of communicating with God through prayer or push you to do it for the first time in your life.

If there is one thing I know, I know that it is only God who can provide the courage, strength, and endurance needed to move forward with life. God is the source of ALL life! Allow the words and scripture references in this book to push you to your knees to connect with a God who is able to take your weaknesses and give you comfort.

This book is comprised of 40 prayers on various topics that were personal to me during the times I was wrestling with these things, and I wrote them. A prayer may cover inner peace to personal growth. The Bible has many symbols connected to the number 40, which is the reason I chose to include only forty journal entries. Jesus was in the wilderness for forty days and forty nights, and Moses walked a wilderness with the Children of Israel for forty years. Other great events occurred, but those two are symbolic to me because, just as Moses led the Children of Israel out of oppression, so does Jesus provide the same freedom for those who are equally oppressed and repressed by struggle and sin. Therefore, I've decided to make the book a book of 40 prayers. I am not saying anything magical will happen; I'm simply saying that it's a good number to model after because several people God used mightily were involved in instances that involved the number 40, and after the number 40 was met, there was freedom. Additionally, you can identify a prayer and scripture and read one a day for a little over a month. Statistics reveal that it takes twenty days to develop a habit. Therefore, if you read one a day, it is possible that you will create a healthy habit of prayer instead of an unhealthy habit of worry.

Last, I titled the book *Simple Prayers for Hurting People* because, for some people who have been broken for so long, it becomes very difficult to find the right words to say or even know where to start. With the table of contents, people can find a prayer that relates to the situation they are in at that very moment or simply find starter words to articulate their brokenness. God still hears the prayers of the broken and hurting, and not only does God hear—God moves and answers! It is my personal prayer that this book pushes you to pray again, pray more, or start praying for the first time! I'll leave you with this scripture before you start:

*"The righteous cry out, and the LORD hears, and delivers them out of all their troubles. The LORD is near to those who have a broken heart, and saves*

*such as have a contrite spirit. Many are the afflictions of the righteous, but the LORD delivers him out of them all."* (Psalm 34:17-19, NKJV)

Terence Lester

June 2011

*Talking to God—Again!*

> *Prayer about Uncertainty*

Dear Lord,

I am fearful. In fact, sometimes my fear of the future bothers me so much that I can't enjoy the present moment. I am uncertain if things will work out for my good. I have experienced so much loss, betrayal, and broken dreams in the past that it is hard to believe there is a future. I know you have a plan for me, but sometimes it's very hard to believe even that. I need your help! I need you to help me see your greatness, power, and grace. I need you to become a tangible comfort and presence to me. I need your spirit to guide me and assure me that you are able to help. I need your spirit to give me the courage I need to confront the fear of the unknown and enjoy all that you have entrusted me with right now. Lord, please help! Even as I pray these words, I feel anxiety and fear knocking on my soul. Father, grant me peace.

Take my cares and concerns and replace them with rest. Give me hope in knowing you love me and will be there for me in ways I need you to be there. Last, Lord grant me strength! Give me strength when I feel both vulnerable and weak. Give me strength when life knocks hope out of me! Give me strength when all signs point to a defeated end. Allow me to be strong in your Son and what Christ has done for me on the cross. Allow me to reflect on his victory and gain strength from that. Allow me to be strengthened in knowing that Christ came to earth to secure my eternity. Allow me to reflect upon him conquering my sin and my having an opportunity to be in right standing with you! Lord, grant me strength and cause me to be sure in all the areas of my life where I feel unsure. Lord, allow my confidence to come from knowing you are with me!

Amen.

*"'For I know the plans I have for you,' declares the LORD, 'plans to prosper you and not to harm you, plans to give you a hope and future. Then you will call on me and come and pray to me, and I will listen to you. You will seek me and find me when you seek me with all your heart."*
Jeremiah 29:11-13, NIV

## *Prayer about Worry*

Dear Lord,

To be honest, what I face has me worried. My finances are running out, my relationships are thinning, and I don't know what you are doing in my life. I pray that you meet me in the midst of my worry. It is clouding my mind to the point that I can't think clearly. Worry has become a lifeline to me. I live off it, breathe through it, and get a pulse from it. And yet, it is killing me. I worry because I am trying to control everything that happens in my life. I want to control all the outcomes that I face, and I know that's not possible. Only you have the power to control the outcomes. All I am responsible for is my part—nothing else! God, grant me the courage to release my grip on what's bothering me! Help me to place it all in your hands and your hands alone.

> *Lord, cause me to focus on the treasures that you have placed before me this day.*

Grant me the courage to accept what is and be confident in knowing that it is okay. Help me to have a perspective change about what's bothering me. Cause me to see the best in what bothers me and not the negatives!

Finally, Lord, cause me to focus on the treasures that you have placed before me this day. Allow me not to think about what I have lost or what I do not have—but push me to enjoy the things that are before my eyes wherever I find myself in life. Thank you for being that type of God who hears even those of us who worry.

Amen.

*"Therefore I tell you, do not worry about your life, what you will eat or drink; or about your body, what you will wear. Is not life more than food, and the body more than clothes? Look at the birds of the air; they do not sow or reap or store away in barns, and yet your heavenly Father feeds them. Are you not much more valuable than they? Can any one of you by worrying add a single hour to your life? And why do you worry about clothes? See how the flowers of the field grow. They do not labor or spin. Yet I tell you that not even Solomon in all his splendor was dressed like one of these. If that is how God clothes the grass of the field, will he not much more clothe you—you of little faith? So do not worry, saying, 'What shall we eat?' or 'What shall we drink?' or 'What shall we wear?' For the pagans run after these things, and your heavenly Father knows that you need them. But seek first his kingdom and his righteousness, and all these things will be given to you as well. Therefore do not worry about tomorrow, for tomorrow will worry about itself. Each day has enough trouble of its own."*
Matthew 6:25-34, NIV

## *Prayer about Doubt*

Dear Lord,

This morning, I woke up with a little doubt. Thoughts in my mind went something like this: "You will not be okay. You will not make it through this! You are a total failure. God isn't working a plan out for you." All those thoughts cause me to go lower and lower on the inside. Moreover, they make me question myself, separate from myself, become very critical and judgmental of myself, and ultimately cause me to doubt you. I need help! I need your help because, when I start to go down, I lose my faith—I lose sight of what you have done for me on the cross through Jesus' sacrifice. I lose sight of how you are transforming me day by day through your Holy Spirit.

Therefore, I need your confidence. I need you to show me that I am secure in my faith with Christ. I want you to show me how I can have full assurance in knowing that you are working on my behalf. Show me that you are real and present. Allow your spirit to comfort me in such a way that it forces me to believe and not doubt. I am tired of being in a place of doubt because it causes me to hurt inwardly. Please, Lord, let me find rest and comfort in knowing that, no matter what I face, you are there! Teach me to trust you and not the negative thoughts that cause me to forsake my faith and not believe you. Reveal to me that you are Lord over all things and will take care of me. I ask you to help me with my doubt today!

Amen.

*"But when you ask, you must believe and not doubt, because the one who doubts is like a wave of the sea, blown and tossed by the wind."*
James 1:6, NIV

> *Prayer for Strength*

Dear Lord,

    This morning, I pray for one thing and one thing alone--strength! On my journey of life, I feel like all my strength has been depleted. I have had a series of events strip away all the inner strength I thought I had. I thought that I had enough willpower and intellect to overpower and outwit what I have been faced with, but somehow I have not been able to. Normally, I am able to manipulate out of situations and overcome them myself. But what I am faced

> *It seems like everything in my life at this point is heavy, even the smallest things.*

with now has knocked the wind out of me. I feel like I am in a boxing ring and life has knocked me down with the referee counting away. I fear that I will not be able to get back up this time around on my own. In fact, every time I try to get up by myself, I can't. It seems like everything in my life at this point is heavy, even the smallest things. Depression, hopelessness, and brokenness have all stolen my strength. I'm exhausted.

On top of my strength being depleted, I feel like I am not worthy anymore. I feel like I am not worth anything at this point. It seems like everything I am around reminds me of the little strength I have left and reminds me of how little value I think I have. I have made mistakes and tried to overcome things alone, and the truth is—I need you! I need your strength that's referred to in the scriptures. I need you to lift me from the boxing ring mat of life and give me strength. I need to feel your love and understand that it is only by your grace, love, and mercy that I am able to overcome all that I face. I need you to empower me through your spirit and comfort my soul. God, become my refuge, my fort, my safety, my rest, and my worth. Fight my battles and show me my worth in Jesus. Lord, give me the courage to bring everything to the cross and lay it down. Give me the strength to say I surrender. Lord, map out a plan for my life and allow me to be in your will. I ask that you do these things and more!

Amen.

*"No temptation has overtaken you except such as is common to man; but god is faithful, who will not allow you to be tempted beyond what you are able, but with the temptation will also make a way of escape, that you may be able to bear it."*
1 Corinthians 10:13, NKJV

## *Prayer about Second-Guessing*

Dear Lord,

I'm in need of your confidence! This morning, I woke up second-guessing myself again. It's like, instead of focusing on what you have down for me in Christ, I look for others to give me words of encouragement, say something nice about me, or compliment me so I feel loved. I'm tired of that because, when the compliments do not come, I feel vulnerable and abandoned. I start to feel worthless and doubt myself and who you've created me to be. Lord, people have become my lifeline, and I am tired of it. I'm tired of seeking approval through people. I'm tired of using things to define me. I need this area of my life broken! I need you to show me how valuable I am in your eyes. I need you to show me that my identity can be found in Christ and his work on the cross. Lord, I need help with my insecurity.

I need you to help me to be secure in you and your love for me! God, allow me to embrace the love you have shown me through the sacrifice that you made through Jesus Christ. Help me to continue taking steps when my thoughts suggest that I should go backwards. God, fill me!

Fill me with thoughts that help me to see the life that you intend for me to live—thoughts of grace, peace, health, and wellness. Help me to see myself the way that you see me. Finally, allow me to have assurance in knowing that my being in a relationship with you is all that matters.

Amen.

*"Being confident of this very thing, that He who has begun a good work in you will complete it until the day of Christ."*
Philippians 1:6, NKJV

## *Prayer for Provision*

Dear Lord,

Today, I come to you with much lack! I lack a plan because the plans I have devised in the past have not worked. I lack opportunity because all the opportunities that I have had have either dissolved or I have not had a break or opportunity yet. I lack in my finances and am scared that I will not have enough to continue the journey of life. I lack in relationships and support, and it has me at times feeling alone, depleted, and empty. God, I lack and am in lack! I need you to provide for me! Provide for me in every area that seems dry. Provide a plan for my life and order my steps. I no longer want to feel lost or as though I'm drifting through life with no direction.

> *I no longer want to feel lost or as though I'm drifting through life with no direction.*

God, provide opportunities for me! Opportunities to grow closer to you, opportunities to use my gifts and talents, opportunities to advance and move forward from the place where I am, and opportunities to enjoy the life you have given me. God, provide for me financially! I need you to pull all your resources together and aid me in living the vision you have given me. I need you to be the main source in my life when it comes to this area. Lord, please provide for me—because, if you do not, it will not happen. Finally, God, provide healthy relationships for my family and me! I have been in a place of loneliness for a while, and I need the community you provide through people. Surround us with people who share your love, joy, safety, and support! Set us in a family where we are accepted, and allow us to feel their embrace. God, fill me with your joy, wholeness, and peace. Let me know that you are present. God, provide! I believe you can, know you can, and trust you can!

Amen.

*"And my God will meet all your needs according to the riches of his glory in Christ Jesus."*
Philippians 4:19, NIV

## *Prayer for a Miracle*

Dear Lord,

Today, I plead with you, God! I am desperate that you hear my side of the story! Never in a million years would I have thought I'd be here. In fact, the plans that I had for my life looked totally different from what I'm currently experiencing. And now, I'm at my lowest point and completely tapped out. I made you my last option by trusting in my abilities and even trusting in the wrong people, and they have led me astray! Please hear me—because I need more than willpower, popularity, resources, and more than what I currently have to overcome what I am facing. I need a miracle! My physical health is not in the best shape because of a lack of self-care. My spiritual health has suffered because of attacks and a lack of personal devotion, and my emotional health has been really low—nearing depression for a number of years now because of past hurts and failures. On top of all that, financially, I'm strapped. The resources I have are starting to run out, and I'm not going to have any more to pull from.

I need a miracle! I need a miracle that would push me to care for myself and see change. I need a miracle that would connect me again to the fountain of your truth and the love you provide through Jesus. I need a miracle from you that will turn my depressed, sorrowful, and gloomy feelings into internal joy! I need that type of miracle that only points to your strength, power, and ability. God, please hear my deepest sorrows. Currently, Lord, I have nothing to my name, and I need you to move these mountains that seem like they will never fall down. Lord, I'm desperate for you to move in my life and on my behalf. I'm desperate for you to perform a miracle in my favor. I need emotional, spiritual, and physical healing. I need you to interrupt natural laws and bring about good in my life for your glory. I need you to send every resource needed for me to live and thrive. God, I beg and plead with you to move on my behalf. God, show me that you are alive and are able to work out the details in my life.

Lord, allow me to be confident in what you have done for me on the cross! God, grant me the peace needed to accept where I am and the endurance to go through what I am going through until my change comes. God, give me fortitude in my spirit to maintain my faith! God, become the miracle I need to live! I love you and need you. Hear my cry and answer my prayers. I believe that you are able to perform miracles.

Amen.

*"God also testified to it by signs, wonders and various miracles, and by gifts of the Holy Spirit distributed according to his will."*
Hebrews 2:4, NIV

## *Prayer about Anxiety*

Dear Lord,

At this point, I feel really anxious! I feel like I am thinking too much about the future, and it is causing me to feel overwhelmed. In fact, my anxious feeling makes me think about how uncertain things are and have been in my life. I have tried things in the past that have failed me, and now I am scared of trusting and believing again. The future causes me to fear and be frightened that what I want to see may never happen at all. I am anxious because I have fear—and I have fear because I am anxious. My heart is heavy because of it, and it hurts. God, I am a fearful, scared, nervous wreck, and I need you to ease my anxiety. I need you to assure me that you have a plan. Give me the courage that replaces fear, and the joy that comforts the pain of anxiety. Help me to see that you are able to restore, build, guide, and help those who are anxious.

> *Help me to see that you are able to restore, build, guide, and help those who are anxious.*

Lord, I ask that you give me freedom from the fear of the future. God, grant me confidence in continuing to strive to make you all I need. God, become the source in my life that gives me life when anxiety feels like it is sucking me dry. Give me confidence in knowing that I can bring all of my cares to you and that you care about them all. Give me the confidence in knowing you have provided a way for me. Remind me that you have a plan for my future and that I do not have to worry. God, show me how I can conquer my anxiety the same way Jesus conquered the grave. Finally, God, give me peace and let me know that I can rejoice that you are with me and haven't left me.

Amen

*"Be anxious for nothing, but in everything by prayer and supplication, with thanksgiving, let your requests be made known to God; and the peace of God, which surpasses all understanding, will guard your hearts and minds through Christ Jesus."*

Philippians 4:6-7, NKJV

## *Prayer for Direction*

Dear Lord,

I need you because today I feel lost. It seems like I have lost my way, and now I need to know which way I should turn or which road I should travel down. Should I continue to travel the road I am traveling, or should I call it quits and go a totally different way? Every turn, decision, and plan I have made in the past has brought me to this place, and this place feels crazy. I feel like I am hanging on by a thread and need strong guidance. I love what I have been pursuing, but the reality is it's hard. It's a hard place, and sometimes I get really scared because I don't know if I'll make it. That's why I feel lost. It literally seems like I am at a fork in the road, and I do not know which way to go.

God, I have even lost confidence in knowing I have what it takes to make a sound decision. Why? Because the journey has been so hard! I'm in desperate need of direction, comfort, and guidance. I'm in desperate need of you showing me which way I should travel or if I should just sit still and do nothing. I need you to show me if I should continue pressing and going or if I should give it all up. I'm confused and need to know your will. I need you to give me clarity of your will for my life at this point and show me the steps to take and what is required to operate and function in the will you have for my life.

Lord, I need you to hurry because I am losing faith that I will ever be found or will know whether I should continue or go a different way. It is causing me so much pain! It seems like everyone around me is moving at a good pace and clearly knows where his or her life is heading. However, I sit, watch, and wonder what I have done wrong to deserve to be in a place where I feel lost. I know I have not been perfect, but I have done the very best I can in maintaining integrity and character. I have even stayed committed to the path I've been on. I really feel like it is all in vain, and I do not want to feel that way.

Please allow me to experience joy in knowing that you are smiling down from heaven on me. Give me confidence in knowing that you still have a plan for my life, and assure me that you can give me the clarity I need to continue moving forward. Feeling lost has me worried, and I need you to ease my *lost-ness* and worry. God, show me that where I am is not a mistake. Reveal to me the lessons that I am supposed to learn with where I am in life and supply me with the right steps to take next. Lord, equip me further for this journey with your divine direction. Give me both peace and contentment to endure where I am until you grant me more opportunities. Lord, allow Jesus to be enough and be my peace until clarity comes.

Amen.

*"The Lord makes firm the steps of the one who delights in him; though he may stumble, he will not fall, for the Lord upholds him with his hand."*
Psalm 37:23-24, NIV

> *Prayer about Rejection*

Dear Lord,

Today, I feel deep rejection. I feel really disappointed because I have received another *no*. It reminds me of the broken promises that I experienced as a child. This alone caused me to feel rejected, and I still wrestle with those broken promises today. Now, every time I hear a *no*, I hear the pain of the child within me waiting, waiting, and waiting, and nothing ever happens. I'm trying my best to move forward, but rejection scares me! I hate hearing *no* because it makes me hurt inside, reminds me of those broken promises, and causes me to feel less than a person. It even causes me to question whether you are there. I have heard *no* all my life, and sometimes—to stop the *nos*—I stop! I stop only to protect myself from the rejection.

However, I want to continue going even when I hear *no* or experience broken promises. I want to hear you scream *yes*

> *God, help me to see my worth even when rejection seems really close!*

through the victory of the cross when *no* is knocking on my heart. I want to dwell on the fact that you approve of me even when I experience let down or hear something opposite of what I was expecting. Lord, help me to face the *nos* with courage and not pull back into a shell every time I am reminded of the pain that I experienced early in life. Help me to see the best in myself even when it seems like life is saying "No." God, cause me to listen to your still small voice of affirmation saying, *"Jesus is enough for you right where you are."* I need you to help me overcome the feeling of rejection! It leaves me vulnerable, sad, depressed, stripped down, and wanting to quit. I don't want to fear anymore! I don't want to quit on myself anymore. I want to stay with the *yes* that I know you provide. God, help me to see my worth even when rejection seems really close! Allow me to live and be free because you have already received me just the way I am.

Amen!

*"If the world hates you, keep in mind that it hated me first. If you belonged to the world, it would love you as its own. As it is, you do not belong to the world, but I have chosen you out of the world. That is why the world hates you. Remember what I told you: 'A servant is not greater than his master.' If they persecuted me, they will persecute you also. If they obeyed my teaching, they will obey yours also."*
John 15:18-21, NIV

## *Prayer about Disappointment*

Dear Lord,

Today, I feel a deep disappointment welling up on the inside of me! For some reason, I feel really negative about where I am in life. I look around, and I am not satisfied. I'm not doing what I would like to do with my career, I have hardly any friends, and I feel alone on top on of all of that. However, I know there is something special about my life—everybody can see it but me. I feel sad and hopeless, and I want it to stop. I do not want to be down any longer. I want freedom from feeling like my world is collapsing. I want freedom from beating myself up with negative thoughts. I want freedom from being imprisoned with pain and hurt. I do not want to place the bar so high anymore that, when I do not achieve or measure up to my perfectionist ways, I am crushed. I'm tired of not measuring up to my own high standards. I am tired of hurting deeply. I am tired of feeling this disappointment.

Help me get past this, Lord. Help me to understand that you are the only one who can ease my deepest wounds and my deepest disappointments. God, help me to realize that it is only you who are able to do the impossible. Not myself, not manipulation, not control, but you! God, allow my heart to be light! Take every care and do not allow the cares of this world to take away my joy. Don't allow the temporary places I find myself in to cause me to forget that you can use all things to work out for good for me and for your glory. God, lead me to scriptures that reassure me that you are able to work miracles on my behalf and that you are able to comfort my deep sorrow. Lord, I'm broken and disappointed, but bringing all that is in my heart to you. Please give me peace! Please meet my deepest needs! Please allow me to be satisfied with how you are satisfied with me. Cause me to reflect on the sacrifice Jesus has made on my behalf. Lord, touch my soul in Christ.

Amen.

*"And remember, I am with you always, to the end of the age."*
Matthew 28:20, NRSV

## *Prayer about Sensitivity and Emotions*

Dear Lord,

My emotions are too much sometimes! In fact, I keep them bottled up so much that they are causing me to implode. I feel really sensitive to all that I have going on inside. It seems like I'm a big wound, and everything that touches me hurts. Lord, that's why I stay closed up

> *God, I no longer want to be a prisoner to my emotions.*

in a shell most times. Living within and never coming out keeps my sensitive emotions protected. However, I know that the walls that I erect are not healthy. In fact, they have me feeling like a lonely wound. God, I no longer want to be a prisoner to my emotions. I no longer want to be sensitive and uptight. I want to heal and let go of the issues, pains, and problems I have held onto for so long. I want to get to a place where I am free to be me and not ashamed of myself and what I have gone through. I want to be strong and have courage.

Lord, give me courage to overcome the shell-like exterior that I erect to keep myself protected. God, cause my heart not to be sensitive to things that remind me of the past. God, transform me so I can bear the fruit that you promise in your scriptures. Allow your spirit to cause me to bear peace, hope, love, joy, long-suffering, and all of the fruit of the spirit that will help me! God, grant me the strength I need to deal with and process things I may be holding onto, and give me the courage to let them go completely. God, allow your Son's sacrifice to stay on my mind. Allow me to see your work in his life, taking him from a crucifixion to a resurrection. Encourage me to know that you are able not only to deal with the cross I carry but to cause me to be changed and resurrected to be made anew. Lord, heal me emotionally and take the cross of the past and make it no more. Allow me to trade it for the cross of Christ and what that fully represents. Transform me and give me the courage to come out of my shell.

Amen.

*"By contrast, the fruit of the Spirit is love, joy, peace, patience, kindness, generosity, faithfulness, gentleness, and self-control. There is no law against such things. And those who belong to Christ Jesus have crucified the flesh with its passions and desires."*
Galatians 5:22-24, NRSV

## *Prayer about Over-Thinking*

Dear Lord,

I need your help with my thought life! Right now, it consumes me. In fact, I tend to over think, dwell on, and be consumed by negative thoughts so much that they cause me to feel burdened. My over-thinking takes me away from things that are pure, just, noble, praiseworthy, and upright and things that I can rejoice about. My negative thought life ruins the way I view this world, you, and sometimes myself! Sometimes, my thoughts push me to believe that no one is there for me, and I am tired of having these thoughts. Your Holy Scripture says that, as a man thinks, so is he.

Well, I have been the by-product of my thought life, and I need you to convict my heart and transform me from the inside out. I need you to help me to dwell on things that are of good report. I need you to make me aware of when I am over-thinking things. Over-thinking is my way of trying to control, figure things out, and remain untrusting. Lord, this is a battle of mine, and I need you! Lord, allow me to reflect on your unchanging nature, what you have sacrificed for the world, and what you are doing in the world through Jesus. Lord, I pray that you and you alone lift me from the rubble of my thoughts and allow me to soar. God, I plead with you and beg you to push me to a place of surrender. I pray that you will cause me to let go and stop over thinking everything.

Everybody does not have a motive, everybody is not out to get me, you have not left me, and things can go right for me! Remind me of the many scriptures that speak about your faithfulness and promises. You are a God who rescues, who remains, who restores, and who recovers. God, rescue me from my over-thinking, restore me from the inside out, and remain with me without giving up on me! I know you are able through Christ, and I know you will through Christ.

Amen

*"For as he thinks in his heart, so is he."*
Proverbs 23:7, NKJV

## *Prayer about Quitting*

Dear Lord,

Today I pray for endurance because I feel like quitting! I have done everything I can possibly do in my own ability to make it happen, and it hasn't yet. It hurts because I feel like I have been getting the short end of the stick for a long time, having to endure set back after set back, and I don't think I can handle it all. I'm at a place where it all seems like a wash, and I have started to question why I started in the first place. Honestly, I feel like quitting, but I know I can't. I feel tapped out and exhausted. I feel like I'm down to my last ounce of strength and on my last card. God, please answer me and tell me why . . . .

Why must I endure all that I have to face? Why hasn't it panned out for me like it has for others? Am I in the wrong? What am I not doing right? Show me a sign, give me hope, give me a lifeline. Anything, Lord! I do not want to quit, give up, or turn away from this! However, closed door after closed door after closed door has me feeling like it's over! It's almost numbing, God, and I need a fresh renewing wind. I need you to lift me from the ash heap and keep me in line with you! Lord, encourage me and show me that it is not over. Make me confident in knowing that you are still working out the details of my life.

Make me confident in knowing that, because Christ has overcome the world, I can too. Show me that, in the midst of hurt and pain, you will deliver. Allow me to understand that the race of life is not given to the swift but to the person who endures to the end. Lord, allow me to be that marathon runner of faith who endures to the end. Allow all that I face to build the faith muscles I need to go onward with life. I need you, Lord, because I am at the end of my rope! I need you, Lord, because, if you do not show up, I am going to fold and throw in the towel. I need you, Lord, because if you do not provide strength, I am going to collapse doing it in my own strength. I do not want to quit, give up, or look back, but I need your help. Allow Jesus to strengthen my heart in the midst of all this pain.

> *Allow me to understand that the race of life is not given to the swift but to the person who endures to the end.*

Amen.

*"Not that I have already attained, or am already perfected; but I press on, that I may lay hold of that for which Christ Jesus has also laid hold of me. Brethren, I do not count myself to have apprehended; but one thing I do, forgetting those things which are behind and reaching forward to those things which are ahead, I press toward the goal for the prize of the upward call of God in Christ Jesus."*
Philippians 3:12-14, NKJV

## *Prayer about Being Misunderstood*

Dear Lord,

It's me again! I hope I'm not bothering you, but I need to talk. I'm weary, and I am down. In fact, right now, I feel like the world is looking at my wounds, pointing the finger, and laughing. "Look at him; he's too different," they are saying. Each stare, funny look, or smart remark cuts me deeply. Why? Because I don't think people understand me or have taken time to really get to know me. That causes me to push people away or close myself up and cut myself off from the world. I feel like you are the only one who understands me and knows me. However, I need help. I need confidence to stand even when it seems like people don't understand me. Whenever I get this feeling, it causes me to close up because I want to protect myself from being hurt by people who are offended with me because they do not understand me or what I'm going through on the inside. Lord, I need you to guide me through this because I know it does not matter what people think about me—only what you think and believe about me.

Help me to shift my focus from people to you. Allow my identity to be rooted in you and nobody else's opinions. God, I need you now, and I need only you. My esteem has been low because I feel so misunderstood. I'm broken and need a new and fresh perspective of how you see me. Allow me to see myself through the work of Christ. Allow my soul to be satisfied that one gave up everything for my relationship with you. Allow me to think of Jesus and his being misunderstood for your sake. Give me the same heart that Christ had, and let me know all is well. I love you for understanding me when it seems like those around me do not. I love knowing that you are all I need and only your opinion of me holds weight. God, I need you, and I need you now.

Amen.

*"Jesus said to them, 'A prophet is not without honor except in his own town, among his relatives and in his own home.'"*
Mark 6:4, NIV

## *Prayer about Isolation*

Dear God,

I'm isolated. I'm alone and lonely. Although I may be in crowds from time to time, I feel no community or connectivity to anyone I'm around. I really feel outcast everywhere I go. Maybe it's because I feel like people don't understand me, or it may be because I have closed myself up and will not allow anyone to get close to me. In fact, the isolation makes me feel worthless, like I am not worth anything! Lord, I need your protection, guidance, and community. Lord, I do not know what to do at this point in my life.

Lord, I need you to connect me with people whom I can be myself around without having my guard up. The way things are going for me, I do not think I will ever have the connectivity that's needed to remove me from this lonely place. I feel like I am going to die in this lonely place, and I do not know what I am going to do. I am willing to open up and step outside my shell. I am willing to move past where I am to connect with people! I just need you to push me to a place of trust because I have not been trusting of others. I have been hurt so much that I have a hard time trusting people and letting them in. Therefore, God, I need you to help me to identify a community and connect with that community. I need you to lead me to people who have your heart and my best interest in mind. I long to laugh, smile, and high-five people without thinking they are talking about me behind my back.

God, I know I have been my own hindrance, and I need it to stop now. I'm hurting alone! I'd do anything to connect with people I can trust. Lord, until you place me in relationship with these people—allow Jesus to become the source of my strength. Allow your Son's sacrifice to remind me that I am connected to a much larger human community. Remind me that I do not suffer alone or by myself. Show me that suffering is a part of the human condition and that Jesus' sacrifice covers it all—even isolation.

> *Show me that suffering is a part of the human condition and that Jesus' sacrifice covers it all—even isolation.*

Amen.

*"A man who has friends must himself be friendly, but there is a friend who sticks closer than a brother."*
Proverbs 18:24, NKJV

## *Prayer about Betrayal*

Dear Lord,

Today, God, I feel betrayed, left, and abandoned! It's hard because, just when you start to trust others and open up, it seems like people pull out a big knife and cut you deeply. It's one of the worst feelings and emotions I have had to wrestle with. It currently has me in a place where I do not trust as easily, which can become extremely unhealthy. This betrayal has me taking everything personally and looking at everyone as a potential suspect to betray me. I do not want to live my life walking on eggshells, thinking everyone is like the betrayer who hurt me. I do not want to take out the pain I have experienced from others on those who could possibly be people who have my best interest at heart. Lord, it hurts though, and I want to protect myself by not trusting anyone—sometimes even you!—because I do not want to be hurt by anyone anymore.

> *God, reveal to me your constant nature. Show me that, when others forsake me, you will never forsake me.*

The occasional betrayal brings up old wounds I have not dealt with yet and even pushes me to run from the love that you provide. This betrayal even has me feeling guilty, shameful, and lonely. It has me questioning my future, my hope, and my faith. It has me deeply bitter, and the bitterness is stealing and robbing me of life! I do not want this cup—please take it from me. I do not want to drink from the bitter cup of not trusting, blaming, and being angry. God, I do not want to lose sight of you being in total control. I want to trust you! However, sometimes I wonder if you will hear me or leave me like others have. God, reveal to me your constant nature. Show me that, when others forsake me, you will never forsake me. God, nourish my starved and depleted soul so that I may be filled with your joy and not be consumed with thinking about the betrayer. To go from thinking someone is for you to finding out that that person did not have your best interest hurts, and I want to move on and not be stuck on this forever.

Help, me to see that there will be many more betrayers, but your Son will never betray me! Show me how to deal with betrayal the way Christ dealt with it. Give me the strength to move forward with my life even when I encounter Judases. Give me the heart to forgive and trust you continually, no matter where I find myself. Allow me to reflect on your Son's sacrifice and give the assurance that, when others walk away, He is still present saying, "I empathize and sympathize with your sufferings."

Amen.

*"Then Judas Iscariot, who was one of the twelve, went to the chief priests in order to betray him to them."*
Mark 14:10, NRSV

# *Prayer for Relationships*

Dear Lord,

I need you right now! Especially, in my relationships. Somehow, they all seem to be suffering right now. People have pulled away from me, others have said nasty things behind my back, and yet others seem not to be as close as I expect them to be. It all sends me into a depression because I lack the understanding why. It hurts not knowing why people change or why the dynamics in various relationships change. Lord, I'm confused. Is it something I have done wrong, or is it something I am not doing right? I need you to reveal this to me. I know each relationship will be time sensitive, be brief to reveal a lesson, or be for a lifetime.

However, I need your help in identifying which ones are which. Help me to see the relationships that are only there to teach me and those that are there for me to continue to build a bridge. Honestly, God, I am torn because, for the first time, I see how much of who I am has been rooted in the relationships around me and not enough in you. God, allow me to get to the point where you are the only relationship that fully satisfies me. God, allow me to be the best person I can be for the natural relationships around me, but allow me to be equally solid in my spiritual relationship with you!

God, I need you to reveal to me the ways in which I can continue to be healthy in the relationships you have given me. Cause me to mature in areas that I bicker about yet grow in the other areas that seem to catch me off guard. Lord, reveal to me my blind spots, those that cause me to wreck relationships and those that hinder me from fully being satisfied in you. God, please help! Allow it all to make sense. If you don't, I may continue to hurt. Lord, please heal the relationships that are on the rocks and remove the relationships that will become thorns. Most important, draw near to me right now because, at this point, you are the only relationship that matters!

Amen.

*"Two are better than one, because they have a good reward for their toil. For if they fall, one will lift up the other; but woe to one who is alone and falls and does not have another to help. Again, if two lie together, they keep warm; but how can one keep warm alone? And though one might prevail against another, two will withstand one. A threefold cord is not quickly broken."*
Ecclesiastes 4:9-12, NRSV

# *Prayer about Sorrow*

Dear Lord,

I am actually glad to be talking to you! It seems like you are the only one who understands what I am wrestling with internally. Right now, I am unhappy and feel sorrow. If joy were a balloon full of excitement, expectancy, and hope, then sorrow is the needle that deflates that balloon. That's exactly what I am feeling at this moment—deflation! Sorrow is stealing the joy I could have, and I am fed up. I'm tired of being sorrowful and having the joy sucked out of me by sorrow. Here's the thing, Lord; I do not know why I am down. I may not have everything going my way, but I do have many things going my way—life, health, supporting relationships, and many other things you've blessed me with.

Why can't I focus on those wonderful things? It seems like all I focus on are things that only create more sorrow—what I've lost, who left, what I have not accomplished, pain I feel, how people misunderstand who I am . . . . All these things become like gas to my fiery sorrow. All these thoughts create my flaming sorrow, and it has to stop. Lord, I desire joy and inner peace. I desire to experience the life that you promise through Christ. I desire to see the light at the end of the tunnel. I long for the moment when all that weighs me down falls to the floor like drops of rain. God, grant me the focus needed to gain a healthier perspective. Help me to find inner peace and joy in knowing that you love me. God, fill my soul and build me up. I feel like I'm at ground zero, and I am in desperate need of reconstruction.

All the things that I thought would provide joy for me have not, and now I am ready to listen and gain the joy that is found in a personal walk with you. Come into me thought life, my heart, and deliver me from the sorrow I have allowed to build up. Allow Christ to free me from the chains of yesterdays, yestermonths, and yesteryears.

Amen!

*"He will wipe every tear from their eyes. There will be no more death or mourning or crying or pain, for the old order of things has passed away."*
Revelation 21:4, NIV

## *Prayer about Emptiness*

Dear Lord,

It seems like lately I have been extremely busy and working too much. In fact, if my soul were similar to a gas tank, I'd say that I am getting close to the "E" line. I'm desperate for a filling from you right now. The journey of life has caused me to run really low on fuel, and before I run out of gas, I need you to show me how to fill myself back up. I read somewhere that life was a long highway and we are like vehicles. To remain fueled, we must figure out our personal filling stations—those places and things that cause us to be filled to travel some more. God, I understand why people say life is a marathon now. It truly is—I used to think I could cover much ground without praying, spending time with you, or even doing fun things that bring me life.

Working too much has stripped my soul's tank dry! I am tired of being really busy and not being productive in my relationship with you. I am tired of waiting until I run low on fuel to know I need rest and fun and to connect with you. I am tired of trying to work really hard to find approval, acceptance, and peace. Why? Because none of it fills my spirit. I'm stressed about trying to make it when you have already made it for me. God, show me how to connect with you and focus on the things that I enjoy to provide fuel for this journey of life. Lord, become the source I need to truly live. Reveal to me the things that drain my soul, and give me the courage to let those things go. Your Son is the bread of life that constantly replenishes, and I want to partake of that relationship. Lord, fill me up and show me those things that are truly important in life.

> *God, show me how to connect with you and focus on the things that I enjoy to provide fuel for this journey of life. Lord, become the source I need to truly live.*

Amen.

*"The Lord is my shepherd; I shall not want. He makes me to lie down in green pastures; He leads me beside the still waters. He restores my soul; He leads me in the paths of righteousness For His name's sake."*
Psalm 23:1-3, NKJV

## *Prayer for Forgiveness*

Dear Lord,

Forgiveness is hard for me, but I know I must do it before the chains of unforgiveness keep me shackled to the past hurts and traumas that I have experienced in life. I am constantly reminded of these hurts when I think about the people who are attached to these hurts and pains. It's hard because I never understood why certain things happened, have not had conversations with those people I need to have had, and have not let them go for the crimes I feel they have committed against me. It's hard to let go of the past because they are wrongdoings, mistreatments, and losses that were inflicted on me, and I did not ask for them to happen. However, although I have a right to be focused on what happened, I hate the way the pain makes me feel.

Unforgiveness has become like bitterness and toxin in my body. It has taken a deep root, and it harms me more than it does those who have offended me. I am a prisoner to my own unforgiveness, and those who caused me hurt are free. God, not only do I need the courage to forgive the people who have done me wrong, I need the courage to model Jesus' example as he forgave those who crucified him unjustly. I need the faith to turn every hurt over to you and give you the opportunity to heal my heart and wounds. It's hard, but I would rather be free and *bitter-less* than remain a prisoner in my own unforgiveness. Lord, I want to take a step forward into the light and leave the bitter darkness of yesteryears.

God, grant me the peace and strength to accept what happened and be okay with what happened. Cause me to know that there is nothing I can do to fix what happened. Cause me to know at this point that I am the only one who needs to be fixed from the inside out. God, take my heart and make it new. Allow me to truly experience the forgiveness you have offered me and grant to people who have wronged me that same forgiveness. Finally, allow Jesus to transform my heart from a heart of stone to a heart of peace. Allow me to follow Jesus forward and not stay stuck in the past.

Amen!

*"For if you forgive men their trespasses, your heavenly Father will also forgive you. But if you do not forgive men their trespasses, neither will your Father forgive your trespasses."*
Matthew 6:14-15, NKJV

## *Prayer for Acceptance*

Dear Lord,

I am opening up more deeply to you today! I long to be accepted. I long to be accepted by the general public, my family, and my friends. I want them all to think that I am a good person and that I have it all together—but that's not the case. The public has not accepted me because I am not famous, some of my friends to do not understand me, and I don't have a very close relationship with my family the way I want. This lack of acceptance leaves me feeling like rubble after a building collapse. Something in me longs to have this acceptance!

Somehow, I think that, if I am praised for how good I am, then maybe it will take away the pain of having to live with myself. I have used the pursuit of acceptance to cover up the fact that I have not accepted myself or believe that you fully accept me—flaws and all. I am tired of pursuing acceptance because it leaves me burned out, depressed, and feeling empty. There is no reward in this type of pursuit. It always ends with a dead

> *God, I need to learn how to love myself unconditionally, the way you love me.*

end. God, I need to learn how to love myself unconditionally, the way you love me. God, show me that you have made me fearfully and wonderfully, even with imperfections. God, show that you loved me so much that you sacrificed your Son for my life and for my acceptance. Lord, I need you! I need you to show me my true worth and value and convict me any time I think that I am not valuable. I want to find acceptance and love from within and by knowing you through Jesus. I want to see my perspective change from needing to be accepted by those around me to knowing all I need is you and you alone.

Lord, I have decided not to try to find love through vain pursuits and by trying to be good enough. I am surrendering my outlook about life, love, and acceptance to you and you alone. God, I thank you for listening and giving me an opportunity to be totally honest with you. Now, I ask that this is enough for me to be whole.

Amen.

*"Everything that the Father gives me will come to me, and anyone who comes to me I will never drive away."*
John 6:37, NRSV

## *Prayer for Rest and Peace*

Dear Lord,

I know what Jesus meant when he told those who were listening that he gives rest and that he wanted to leave a peace that the world does not offer. Why? Because I am overwhelmed. I am overwhelmed with all of my responsibilities, the pressures of my own expectations, and many things that have me stressed out. Oh, how do I desire that rest your Son spoke of—but somehow I do not think I can lay everything down at his feet. I wrestle with knowing whether Jesus will really exchange peace for my burdens or cause me to be stressed out even more. All of the things pulling me away from true peace and rest are not even worth it. I guess I have been frustrated with these things for so long that I don't think I can have a life outside of worrying about them or trying to toil to correct them myself.

However, I am tired. I am tired of being in this place where I am carrying. I truly want to relieve my mind by knowing that Jesus did not come to burden me more. I am ready to take on the light yoke that Christ offers. Carrying all that I am carrying keeps me up at night, steals my joy, and causes a struggle in my soul. I need you, God, to lift from me the burdens I have been carrying and give me a true rest in my soul. A rest that will cause me to be at peace in my mind. A rest that will cause me to stop stressing about the small things. A rest that will replace the heavy workload and whisper to me, *"Rest and live."* Allow me to embrace the idea that your Son literally came to earth to free me from the oppression I am under. Allow me to fully know that I can drop everything and drink from the fountain you provide—the fountain of rest. Lord, I am ready to trade in the cares of this world and everything that is pressing me for the rest and peace you provide.

Amen.

*"Come to me, all you who labor and are heavy laden, and I will give you rest."*
Matthew 11:28, NKJV

## *Prayer about People Pleasing*

Dear God,

I'm coming right out and saying it: I am a people pleaser. I have become very codependent over the years, and it is bothering me. It's like I am addicted to rescuing, helping, and trying to control people I think need my help. For some reason, I get life from being addicted to other people's needs. However, it hurts! As I do all I can to help others, it seems like I get the short end of the stick.

> *Lord I am tired of performing and putting on a show and not staying true to myself and my feelings.*

How? Because the people don't do anything to reciprocate what I have done for them. I become easily attached and then extremely frustrated. Instead of allowing people to make their own decisions about choosing whether they will be in a relationship with me, I jump the gun and try to please people to be accepted.

In addition, Lord I am tired of performing and putting on a show and not staying true to myself and my feelings. It all has me bitter inside, and I'm not sure if I can please people anymore. It comes with too many job descriptions, and I do not think I am strong enough to fill all those roles anymore. Pleasing people has become like a prison for me, and I am both the guard and the prisoner. I am ready to stop pleasing people because it gets me nowhere and returns absolutely nothing but things to do to try to measure up to people's expectations of me. Lord, I am ready to seek to please only you and show compassion only toward those who truly need it. I am ready to stop giving so much of myself to others to try to please them and gain acceptance. I am ready to give up trying to be satisfied in my soul by pleasing others. I am ready to give up trying to control others through my pleasing. Even more than that, God, I am ready to stop trying to accomplish and achieve so much to get people to accept me! This has been the worst type of pleasing I have done. Period.

    Lord, as I take this step forward, give me courage to surrender and let go of this addiction. Lord, help me to recover so much of myself that I have spread around. Give me the strength to stop trying to gain love through useless deeds, giving to needs that I was never asked to give to, or get involved in things I was never asked to get involved in. Up to this point, it has caused me to be sick, and I am letting go. From this day forward, I am allowing you to break this awful habit. Do it, Lord, and allow Jesus Christ to be everything to me. Remind me that Jesus never requires that I do anything but come forward and accept him. Increase my relationship with you through Christ.

Amen.

*"Am I now trying to win the approval of human beings, or of God? Or am I trying to please people? If I were still trying to please people, I would not be a servant of Christ."*
Galatians 1:10, NIV

## *Prayer about Busyness*

Dear Lord,

"Spread thin" is an understatement of what I am feeling right now! I have taken on too many responsibilities, and I feel like I am drowning with all of these items. Honestly, Lord, I had kept myself busy because it helps me to cope with the pain that I have inside! Somehow, I think, the busier I am, the better the pain will be—but that's a lie. Why? Because now I am busy and I still have the inner pain. "If I could only achieve more, then I'd be alright," I thought. If I could just continue to climb the mountain of achievements, then it would substitute for the confusion, depression, and agony I feel within. I have now come to realize that being busy does not equate to being healthy.

In addition, I have discovered that being busy does not produce the type of peace I thought it would produce. In fact, being busy has become an enemy to my soul and an enemy to my relationship with you. God, I need your help. I need help reducing my responsibilities, creating room in my life, and being okay with where I am. I need your help confronting the things that I have run from for my entire life. I want to be whole, God, and I know you have the power to make me whole. I know that you can strip away those things that are low priority and heal my heart after removing what I need to let go. God, make me healthy and reveal to me ways in which I can heal. I am surrendering to you right now! I am giving up the pursuit to achieve to meet with you and to sit with myself.

God, show me that solitude is healthy and a way I can reconnect with myself and dialogue with you. God, even as I am praying, I feel the load is lightening. Why? Because I am confessing so much to you! I feel courage coming over me in areas that I can let go. I do not want to repeat the same mistakes my whole life. Cause me to experience true life with a light load and simple things in life. Allow me to be content with a few things and not be overwhelmed with many things. Show me that following Christ doesn't have to be heavy and loaded down, but light and easy. Remind me that Jesus was content with a few things while on earth but still made an impact. Give me the courage to be content like

> *I have discovered that being busy does not produce the type of peace I thought it would produce.*

Jesus and place my life totally in your hands. God, allow me to decide not to be busy anymore!

Amen.

*"Be still, and know that I am God!"*
Psalm 46:10, NKJV

# *Prayer about Blaming*

Dear God,

Blame may be holding me back and keeping me a prisoner to unforgiveness and things that have happened in the past. I have started to notice how I blame people for things that I am dealing with inside. When I hurt, I blame people. When I am not progressing the way I think I should progress, I blame people. When I feel alone, I blame people! When I am angry, I blame people. And, if I can be really truthful—I have given people too much power over me, and I am sick of it. It has become the easiest answer for the problems I face in my life. It's not healthy and has me sick inside.

It has me sick because, instead of turning to you for guidance, answers, or wisdom, it causes me to push myself away from you and those who really care. God, I am tired of blaming others for where I am in life and for what I do not have. Blaming has even caused jealousy and envy to breed in my heart. When other people have what I do not have, I somehow blame them for why I do not have what I think I deserve. I want freedom from this now. I want to wake up and accept everything that is in my life—the things I desire and the things I loathe. God, give me the courage to accept my reality and stop the blaming.

Give me the strength to be at peace with all that I have had to endure and show me it is a part of the journey of life. Grow me in tremendous ways God! Cause me to seek your face before pointing the finger at someone else. Grant me the strength that Jesus had when he did not blame his persecutors but simply said, *"Permit even this."* Give me the courage to say, *"Not my will but your will be done."* Lord, help me! I no longer want to play the blame game or even give people that much weight in my life. I pray that you, God, will change my heart from blaming to trusting that you and you alone have a plan for me in all seasons of life.

Amen.

*"Do not conform to the pattern of this world, but be transformed by the renewing of your mind. Then you will be able to test and approve what God's will is—his good, pleasing and perfect will."*
Romans 12:2, NIV

## *Prayer about Envy and Comparison*

Dear Lord,

I'm convinced that the thing that paralyzes me and hinders me from moving forward is envying what other people have and even comparing myself to others. It causes me to reject myself and place other people before me. That's not healthy or good because it stops me. Lately, I have been in comparison mode. I look at what I do not have and what others do have, and secretly, it causes me to dislike my life. It makes me feel horrible inside. Why? Because it causes me to not like and love myself as I should. It hurts because, not only does it spread through my body, but it makes me think that I will not have a future. It has even become a full-time job to compare myself to others—and I might add it is very tiring.

Lord, I am tired of comparing myself to others and not being grateful for what you have given me. I am reminded of the man with the one talent in the scriptures who went and buried his talent. I do not want to be that person! I do not want to compare and envy so much that it causes me to take all that you have placed inside of me and go bury it. Lord, I desire to love myself, see myself the way that you see me, and focus solely on what you are able to do. Lord, help me to realize that I am where I am supposed to be in life and allow that to be enough for me to be satisfied. God, allow me to focus more on what you have done for me and not what I can do for myself. Give me the right perspective about my life. Allow me to take whatever you have given me and give it back to you by being a great steward over it. Lord, convict my heart and cause me to stop comparing myself to others and rejecting myself by trying to live vicariously through what others have. It does not work. I am ready to let go and fully accept you and the work you've done for my freedom. Allow me to fully experience the love you provide through Christ.

Amen

*"For where you have envy and selfish ambition, there you find disorder and every evil practice."*
James 3:16, NIV

## *Prayer to Find My Way Home*

Dear Lord,

One of my favorite authors wrote about finding your way home, and I never fully understood it until I realized that I have been seeking life in everything outside of me—in relationships, in material things, in conversations, in expectations, in blaming, in unforgiveness, in problems, in everything external. All of this external searching has caused me to wander away from who I truly am and make myself empty of my own presence. Finding your way home is about turning inward and upward—inward to search within to find inner peace and upward to solidify that peace. Living in the externals has caused me on several occasions to feel extremely lost about the direction I am taking in life. That's how I feel now because, instead of seeking myself within and in you, I have come to a place where the search for myself in everything external no longer fuels, directs, or satisfies me. It does not provide peace, encouragement, assurance, affirmation, identity, or any of the other things that I need in my life at this point. Lord, I need to return home. Please accept me with open arms the way the father did when his prodigal son decided to return home.

      Lord, give me the courage to accept myself, love myself, and welcome myself back home from living outside of myself for so long. Lord, allow me to find my true identity in you and leave everything else behind. Allow my roots to grow deeply in knowing you and the sacrifices you have made for me. Allow me to discover that what I have been searching for all along has never been in the externals but has been inside all along. God, strengthen my confidence and convict me every time I think about finding myself outside in external things. Remind me each time I try that you are enough for me because you are in me.

Amen.

*"For indeed, the kingdom of God is within you."*
Luke 17:21, NKJV

> ## *Prayer about Depression*

Dear Lord,

  Today clouds are present again, and I am starting to wonder if they will ever clear. In fact, the clouds are causing me to see life through dark lenses. Everything looks dismal—relationships, where I am in life, my hope, and my future. Why am I here? Tell me how I got here, God. I never asked to be depressed, but I find myself here again. My depression has even caused me to see you in a small light. It hurts because I desperately long to see the sunshine beyond the clouds. But I can't yet. Every time I encounter something that reminds me of my thinking I am worthless or rejection or betrayal, I find myself right here.

  I'm tired of this place because the birds are not chirping, the clouds are not white, and the sky is not blue. I am ready to see the sunshine that you have for my life. I am ready to release the glow I know I have inside of me. I am ready to get past the pain and open up instead of allowing my negative thoughts to wrestle me to the ground. I am ready to get rid of my negative thinking syndrome and embrace the light you provide through Christ. Lord, I need your help taking the first step toward the light. I need your help believing that, as I take steps toward the light, you will take steps toward me. Allow the passage from James to flood my heart when it says, *"if we draw near to you, you'll draw near to us."*

God, give me the courage to speak your truth when that which is an enemy to me whispers lies. God, show me that your Son, Jesus Christ, has come to lift me from the grave of depression and that he cares for me. Lord, I am willing to take the first step today toward the light, and I need you to meet me half way. Cause me to be both hopeful and encouraged. You are the way and the way out, and I desire to take that way. I love you and look forward to seeing the light you provide.

Amen.

*"Weeping may endure for a night, But joy comes in the morning."*
Psalm 30:5, NKJV

## *Prayer for Counsel*

Dear Lord,

I'm back again, and I'm desperate for your counsel and guidance. I've made some choices that have put me in a really uncomfortable position. The position is hard because I feel stripped and powerless over what I face. Maybe I moved too soon and didn't allow you to guide me or make a way for me! Maybe I was just too impatient. I saw, it looked good, and I jumped. I did not even consult you. I thought I'd just include you on the decision after I made everything work out they way I wanted. What an awful idea.

I moved without wise counsel and now find myself at a crossroads. More than anything, I need your counsel. Lord, it hurts to know that I moved ahead of you and even ahead of myself.

> *I need you to surround me with individuals who have overcome this place and will have the words to share with me on how to get out of this place.*

God, I need you to counsel me through this awkward place. I need you to surround me with individuals who have overcome this place and will have the words to share with me on how to get out of this place. God, I am tired of moving ahead of you and not giving you time to make things clear to me. Lord, I need your clarity. I need the lessons that will equip me to choose the right path and direction. Use my unwise decisions, bad judgment, and unhealthy ways to provide principles I can apply to where I am now. Lord, use the brokenness that I exposed through my hastiness for your glory and my good.

      Use every wrong decision to push me closer to you and cause me to grow internally. Allow me to seek Jesus the way the woman with the *issue* did after she had exhausted everything in her life. Give me the courage to seek you to the point where I touch you and you transform me from the inside out. God, change the way I think, increase my patience, and order my steps. Lord, I pray that you and you alone give me the guidance from where I am now.

                                                  Amen.

*"The counsel of the Lord stands forever, the plans of his heart to all generations."*
Psalm 33:11, ESV

> *Prayer for Wisdom*

Dear God,

Wisdom has not been present in every aspect of my life. Of course, I know a lot of information, people have advised me and I accepted their advice, and I can even articulate many wise things clearly and precisely. However, I need help. I need help because I do not apply everything I know all the time. Sometimes the information becomes head knowledge only, and at this point in my life, I need to see ways in which I can apply all the knowledge I have.

In fact, information has been a blessing and a curse to me. Too much information has become head knowledge, which is good but sometimes does not come out in my behavior. I need the wisdom that Solomon prayed for when you asked him what he wanted. I need applied wisdom—the wisdom that moves one past the collection of data to a place where the data or information is lived out. God, allow the information to seep down into my heart and transform me. Push me to live the life I know about in every area of my life, not just a few places. God, grant me the wisdom to continue to grow and develop as a follower and as your child. Cause me to see my areas of weakness and not overlook them, but address them by applying what I already know. God, allow me to bear fruit in those areas and make wise decisions as I continue to journey forward in life. I believe that you are able to do these things and more.

Amen.

*"If any of you lacks wisdom, let him ask God, who gives generously to all without reproach, and it will be given him."*
James 1:5, ESV

## *Prayer for Family*

Dear Lord,

Today, I am grateful. I am grateful that you have given me my own personal family. I am grateful that I can look into my family's eyes and see love. I am grateful that you have given me something to steward in an area that I feel I have been deprived of most of my life. God, I pray that you will develop me in ways that I have not fully developed in because of my upbringing and grant me the maturity to love my family with the love that you have shown me. God, provide for my family, keep my children safe, and cause us to be unified and not divided. Protect us against every attack that an enemy tries to throw our way and bless us with your peace, serenity, and love.

> *I am grateful that I can look into my family's eyes and see love.*

God, make us a blessing to those around us and cause us to be good stewards over everything that you entrust to us. God, allow me not to repeat what I saw growing up and allow me to heal from the family hurts that I experienced in my past. God, become a father to me, a mother to me, and a friend to me. Nourish my soul with affection and support so I may give my family love out of the overflow of what I have received from you. Allow me to model Christ to my children and love my wife like your Son loves the Church. Allow me know to that you have a larger family that I am connected to through Jesus and that you care for those who are isolated, confused, and alone. God, show me that you set the lonely in families. I love you and thank you for giving me a family of my own. God, I just pray that you keep me strong so I can be strong for my family.

Amen

*"For if someone does not know how to manage his own household, how will he care for God's church?"*
1 Timothy 3:5, NKJV

## *Prayer for Hope*

Dear Lord,

I'm back again. I started off this day really hopeful but have had several things happen unexpectedly, and now I'm experiencing a little doubt. It's funny how easy it is to slide down the mountain of hope into the valley of despair. God, my prayer is simple. Lift me up from this place of hopelessness. Allow the doubt I feel right now to subside. Better yet, give me the courage to look upward, not to focus on what happened but what can become of what happened. Allow me to see that you have a plan for what happened unexpectedly today. Although I do not know what exactly happened, cause me to hope in you! Increase my faith in ways that cause me to walk trusting you and being okay with not knowing how things will pan out. God, grow me in ways that stretch me!

Additionally, Lord, remind me of your Son's faith in the garden when he was sweating drops of blood and preparing to go to the cross. Remind me of his faith, hope, and courage to believe you when he felt hopeless and alone. God, give me the strength to hope in you when I am sweating drops of hopelessness and cause me to believe that you will be with me know matter what happens. Push me to know that greatness can come out of adversity and that you can bring yourself glory out of the bleakest situations. God, give me hope! Allow my heart to be totally encouraged and show me that this too shall pass and not plague me all of my days. Give me mercy and give me grace.

Amen.

*"Be of good courage, and He shall strengthen your heart, all you who hope in the Lord."*
Psalm 31:24, NKJV

## *Prayer for Healing*

Dear Lord,

Today, I ask that you heal my body—emotions, body, and spirit. I am in desperate need of a cleansing through seeking you and detoxing. I have consumed so much bad food, negativity, and brokenness that I'm not aligned. I need a balancing to happen within. Therefore, I am asking you to bring about a healing. Heal me from depression, heal the illness that plagues my body, and heal my spirit. Help me to rid myself of all harmful toxins that caused me to remain wounded. Lord, I am seeking you because I know you have the power to bring about the very inner healing I need to move forward. I am tired of being a wounded healer—a person who can heal others but cannot heal himself.

> *God, I am hitting the reset button and turning everything about me over to your care.*

At this very moment, I place myself in your hands and ask that you become the physician I need to experience healing. I pray that you will restore, rejuvenate, and revive me. God, I am hitting the reset button and turning everything about me over to your care. Cause me to take care of myself and be healthy in mind, body, and spirit. God, heal me from the inside out and allow all the healing that takes place within to show and shine brightly on the outside. God, allow me to have the faith that you are able to heal me if you choose to. Comfort me in knowing that you care for me while I battle the illnesses I face. However, I am desperate, Lord. I need a touch from you, a word from you, and a restoration from you! You are my hope, and I ask that you move through the power of your spirit.

Amen.

*"Is anyone among you sick? Let them call the elders of the church to pray over them and anoint them with oil in the name of the Lord. And the prayer offered in faith will make the sick person well; the Lord will raise them up. If they have sinned, they will be forgiven."*
James 5:14-15, NIV

## *Prayer to Let Go*

Dear Lord,

Today, I ask that you give me the courage to fully surrender and let go. Allow me to let go of trying to control every little detail about my life. Why? Because every time I try to control my life, I end up seeing how powerless I am and how fragile I am against life. My controlling nature causes me not to trust you fully sometimes, and I do not want to be in a place where I do not trust you. At this very moment, I am surrendering my plan to you because I need your plan more than mine! My plan is not working at all and has only revealed to me that I am weak. Lord, help me. Help me to reorganize my life and build again brand new. Give me a new start and give me the courage to let go of the past.

God, give me solace in knowing that where I have been does not define me, but where you are able to take me does. God, allow me to experience another new birth—being born anew from the inside. Cause me to remember the new life I once experienced and to encounter that new life again. God, show me how to trust you! Restore the joy of my salvation and cause me to believe that your plans for my life are better than my own. God, at this moment—I surrender.

Amen.

*"Trust in the Lord with all your heart, and lean not on your own understanding; in all your ways acknowledge Him, And He shall direct your paths."*
Proverbs 3:5-6, NKJV

# *Prayer of Confession*

Dear Lord,

I am no saint, and I believe you already know that, but I wanted to let you know I know too. In recent years, I have lied, been angry, manipulated, and even been envious. All of it comes from my wanting to embrace the flesh instead of the spirit. God, I confess my sins and shortcomings and ask that you forgive me. Forgive me for the hurt and damage I've caused. Forgive me for not listening to you or the people that you sent my way to warn me. Forgive me for the times I wanted more of the world than more of your spirit. Forgive me for breaking several promises that I made to you on the spur of the moment. Lord, I confess and need your grace. You said through the beloved John that, if I confess, you would cleanse me in ways I need cleansing.

> *God, I confess my sins and shortcomings and ask that you forgive me.*

Now, Lord, cleanse me! I invite you into the mess of my life and ask that you make things right within me. I ask that you give me the courage not to beat myself up and see that you are not whipping me either. God, cause me to know how much you love me instead of how much you are disappointed in my ways ad behaviors. God, invade my heart, mind, and life and give me a refreshing. Let me know that it is okay to fall and get back up again. Remind me of how Peter was restored after denying Jesus multiple times. God, use the wreckage of my life to impact the lives and hearts of others after you have restored me. I confess, and I receive your forgiveness.

Amen.

*"If we confess our sins, He is faithful and just to forgive us our sins and to cleanse us from all unrighteousness."*
1 John 1:9, NKJV

## *Prayer about Conflict*

Dear Lord,

Why do I constantly find myself in conflict—either with other people, with you, or with myself? The conflict that I go through sometimes does not help at all. Lord, today my prayer is simple. Help me stop starting conflicts and give me the wisdom not to allow conflict to get inside of me and cause me to sink. God, allow my response to conflict not to be with rage and reactionary, but allow me to respond to conflict. God, I desire not to live a life without conflict but to have the wisdom to know how to respond to conflict as it arises.

God, deal with my heart and cause me to grow in the areas that cause me to start conflict and give me the strength to withstand that heat of conflict when it comes my way unexpectedly. Allow my choice during conflict to be pleasing in your sight, filled with grace, and seasoned with humility. God, grow me in the area of conflict.

Amen.

*"A gentle answer turns away wrath, but a harsh word stirs up anger."*
Proverbs 15:1, NIV

## *Prayer about Grief*

Dear Lord,

Loss hurts, and it has hurt me. Recently, I have lost friendships, respect, material things, health, dreams, and hopes. I don't know how to deal with it. Sometimes I get caught in a cycle of denial, anger, bargaining, and depression. But I know none of those can recover what has been lost. I know I must accept to move onward, but sometimes it is hard to accept things that you think you should not lose. Tell me, God, why do we lose things without clear answers sometimes? Why do you allow certain things we perceive as evil to happen? Why do you allow it when you know that your creation will grieve? I am waiting on you to answer, God, because I want to know. I have grieved for a long time, and I need you to help me out of this grief.

> *Give me the strength to release what has died into your hands, knowing that you have the power to resurrect what has died.*

Don't allow me to grieve and then leave me in the grief. Don't allow my back to be up against the wall and not supply me with the strength needed to overcome the blows from what is an enemy to me. I need you now—not tomorrow, not next week or next month, but right now.

God, help my heart and give me the courage to accept what you have already accepted about my life. Lord, give me the courage to look toward you like Mary and Martha after they lost their living brother and your friend. Give me the strength to release what has died into your hands, knowing that you have the power to resurrect what has died. Allow me not to drown in grief but to move to acceptance and letting go. I love you and know that you are able to deliver me. Hurry, because I want to leave the prison of grief. Allow me to walk out of the grave with Jesus and not stay there grieving. I love you, Lord.

Amen.

*"Casting all your care upon Him, for He cares for you."*
1 Peter 5:7, NKJV

## *Prayer for Endurance*

Dear Lord,

As I look back over my journey, I am inspired that you have allowed me to cover much ground. You allowed me to overcome obstacle after obstacle. You were there for me even when I was not there for me. You literally carried me when I collapsed and quit. Therefore, today, I ask that you give me a second wind. I pray that you give me the strength and courage needed to endure the next stretch of miles I must travel. Give me the endurance needed not to collapse or fall down again. God, build me up and allow me to tap into your strength. When I look back over my life and what you have given me strength to do, it reveals to me that you have built me for this journey. Remind me of that when I fall to my knees; remind me of that when I can't see how taking another step will help. Remind me that this race is not run with a quick sprint but by taking step after step and following your lead.

Amen.

*"Therefore, since we are surrounded by such a great cloud of witnesses, let us throw off everything that hinders and*

*the sin that so easily entangles. And let us run with perseverance the race marked out for us"*
Hebrews 12:1, NIV

## *Prayer about Process*

Dear Lord,

I never knew that it would take this long to accomplish the goals I am trying to accomplish. I thought, because I am talented, skilled, and knowledgeable, that it could happen overnight. Oh, how I was wrong! This is messing with my faith, faithfulness, trust, and patience, and it hurts. It hurts deeply because I believe so much in my mission and have not seen the fullness of it yet. It hurts because it involves tons of time and process. I'm not a big fan of process, God. I cannot stand it, but I know that you allow us all to go through and grow through process.

One of my mentors recently told me, *"Terence, God is more concerned with the work he is doing in you than the work you'll do on the outside."*
Ouch! That's how I feel—as though you are working on me from the inside out. However, I still need your help. I need you to help me remain faithful,

> *Lord, you know where I am, what I need, and what you are working out within me.*

consistent, and committed to the goals that you have given me for the long haul and not give up on them when things are not moving as fast as I would like. I need you to grow me in my patience, faith, and confidence. Cause me to choose obedience over microwave progress. Lord, you know where I am, what I need, and what you are working out within me. Therefore, comfort me in this process. Cause me to reflect on Joseph as he endured a process of thirteen years before you freed him from prison for crimes he did not commit. Allow me to realize why you have me going through what I am going through and show me what areas you want me to grow and develop in. Lord, I trust you in the process, and I give you the cares, impatience, and disbelief I am wrestling with. Help me through this process!

Amen.

*"My brethren, count it all joy when you fall into various trials, knowing that the testing of your faith produces patience. But let patience have its perfect work, that you may be perfect and complete, lacking nothing."*
James 1:2-4, NKJV

## *Prayer for Personal Growth*

Dear Lord,

I am glad you have given me opportunities to share with you exactly how I am feeling without judgment. I thank you for being a God who understands the cries of your children. I am starting to see some fruit—fruit of opening up, fruit of forgiveness, fruit of letting go, fruit of taking steps that I have not been able to take—and the list goes on. However, I am realistic, God. I know growth happens every day—not in one day!

And I guess that's what I want to talk to you about. I need you to keep me on the path that I am on and continue to grow me. I need you to remind me through your Spirit every time I feel like turning back and shrinking down to what I used to be. I desire a growth that lasts until I make my transition. I desire to grow in all the areas I still struggle in but realize that perfection is not my end goal—striving to be MORE like Jesus is. God, I love you and will continue to bring every care to you, every concern to you, and every problem to you. Why? Because I know that you and you alone answer hurting people!

Amen.

*"But grow in the grace and knowledge of our Lord and Savior Jesus Christ. To him be glory both now and forever! Amen."*
2 Peter 3:18, NIV

## *Walking with God through Christ*

After reading these prayers, do you feel like you should take a step and make Christ your Savior? I know it is a tough decision, but the gospel says that Jesus came to earth to provide the freedom and hope we all desire. It says that Jesus reconciles us to God and ourselves. Do you want life? I do not know where I'd be without a God walking with me even in the midst of my suffering and pain. Is this you? Are you in pain? Well, here are five simple steps to start your new journey if you want to receive Christ:

1. Admit you are a sinner and need a savior. You can do this quietly by simply saying, "God, I know I am in sin, and need you to recue me from it."
2. Confess and repent—admit those things you have done.
3. Believe that Jesus Christ died for you and rose again.
4. Confess Jesus as Lord and Savior!

Last, pray this simple prayer:

*"Dear God, I am broken and nowhere near where I should be with you. However, I want to be in that place. I believe that Jesus died on the cross to pay the price for my sins, and I know you can restore me by giving me new life. No longer do I have to live in guilt and shame. I receive Jesus as my Lord and Savior. Amen!"*

From here, your next step is simple: Search for an awesome Bible-believing church where there are real people with real problems who aren't afraid to admit and confess that. I believe getting plugged into this type of community will cause you to grow in ways that you desire. Additionally, I encourage you to starting reading through the gospels in the New Testament. They will help you understand the life and ministry of Jesus. I hope this book has helped you to reconnect with a God who hears hurting people in the midst of their pain!

*"If you declare with your mouth, 'Jesus is Lord,' and believe in your heart that God raised him from the dead, you will be saved. For it is with your heart that you believe and are justified, and it is with your mouth that you profess your faith and are saved."*
Romans 10:9-10, NIV

## *About the Author*

Passionate . . . effective . . . determined . . . sincere . . . focused . . . radical . . . committed! These are only a sampling of glowing comments following encounters with a unique and powerful personality.

A fitting news headline might read, "BAD BOY GONE GOOD!" You see, the Terence B. Lester story could well have emerged as the recapitulation of another life thrown away. This same story could have easily contributed to growing negative statistics about young men.

From a troubled youth in the midst of danger, chaos, and trial, Lester found a missing piece that has created a beautiful portrait of change. God has caused that piece to change his life—FOREVER! Now, he is on fire for Jesus and on a mission to reach the young and old, lost, confused, hopeless, troubled, and those who might question whether there is any good in this life for them.

He is gratefully married to Cecilia L. Lester, a woman who stands ably by his side and takes great pride in being the father of their beautiful daughter, Zion Joy Lester. Lester holds a Bachelor of Theology from ABC and a Master of Education degree from Liberty University and is the author of a number of books.

Experiences as an educator in a public school setting have contributed greatly to his ability to discern hopelessness, despair, and dysfunction within the emerging generation. Lester knows exactly what it will take to reach them: boldness, sincerity, encouragement, and transparency. He has become a much sought-after speaker, with over 1,000 engagements in elementary, middle, and high schools; colleges and universities; many churches; Christian and non-Christian television programs; and several book festivals. In addition, he has been featured in several publications.

Equipped with an unusual ability to relate to his audience, it takes only moments for them to realize that this man is FOR REAL! Lester reminds the world that there is absolutely NOTHING too hard for God! He comes to stand in partnership and agreement with ALL those who love God and are unwilling to give up on a younger generation.

## Contact Information

Terence Lester is available for speaking engagements, book signings, workshops, and conference participation. You may go online and request Terence Lester's services or books on the World Wide Web at terencelester.com, send an email to contact@terencelester.com, or call 404-955-8033

*Thanks for your support!*

# *Additional Books*

*Getting Past Stuck* by Terence B. Lester
ISBN-10: 0615606989
ISBN-13: 978-0615606989

*Identity Theft* by Terence B. Lester
ISBN-10: 0692003339
ISBN-13: 978-0692003336

*U-Turn: The Teenage Turnaround* by Terence B. Lester
ISBN-10: 1599164094
ISBN-13: 978-1599164090

Made in the USA
Middletown, DE
12 August 2019